YOUR BEST YEAR EVER

7 simple ways to shift your thinking and take charge of your life

Copyright © 2015 by Kelly Exeter

All rights reserved.

Published in Australia by Swish Publishing, Perth, Western Australia.

www.swishpublishing.com.au

National Library of Australia
Cataloguing-in-Publication entry

Author: Exeter, Kelly M., 1977- author.

Title: Your best year ever: 7 simple ways to shift your thinking and take charge of your life / Kelly Exeter.

ISBN: 9780992441623 (paperback)

Notes: Includes bibliographical references.

Subjects: Self-actualization (Psychology). Self-help techniques. Happiness. Life skills.

Dewey Number: 158.1

Printed in the United States of America

First Edition

Cover Design: Adrian Bollig • Book Design: Swish Design
Author photo: Robyn Petta

*To Ant – for being you.
And for loving me, even though I am
a massive pain in the arse.*

CONTENTS

Introduction 1

Chapter 1:
A different way of looking at yourself 7

Chapter 2:
A different way of looking at time 15

Chapter 3:
A different way to approach decision making 25

Chapter 4:
A different way to approach bad habits 33

Chapter 5:
A different way to face your fears 41

Chapter 6:
Changing our definition of a 'connected' life 51

Chapter 7:
A different way to approach your life 59

So What Now? 69

References and Credits 75

Acknowledgements 77

Thank You 79

YOUR BEST YEAR EVER

7 simple ways to shift your thinking and take charge of your life

KELLY EXETER

INTRODUCTION

"So long, farewell, don't let the door hit you on the arse on the way out ..."

That was a friend's 'goodbye to the year' message a couple of years ago and I can tell you right now, she wasn't the only one.

Everywhere I looked at the end of that particular year (and years since), I was seeing disillusionment and frustration; people slowly being crushed by the weight of 'one thing after another'.

Things like: issues at work; betrayal by those they trusted; behavioural challenges with children; relationship troubles. All things that could be dealt with if they arose one at a time but for many people they seemed to be occurring en masse.

In a nutshell, overwhelm seemed to be the rule rather than the exception. I remember one friend saying she felt life was something just happening to her and all she could do was react.

That reactive feeling, it's horrible isn't it? It's also one I was once very familiar with.

The 2010 version of me was running a small but rapidly growing graphic design business, building three houses, and experiencing motherhood for the first time.

My business was the main problem. I had neglected to set it up to run without me in it so when my baby was born, I didn't have even one day off. (To the mortification of my clients, I was sending invoices from hospital the day after he was born.) And like many small businesses, we were running right on the line between black and red so my staff and I were working insanely hard for little financial reward.

Additionally, I was a creative person whose days featured little opportunity to be creative because I was so caught up in the soul-destroying minutiae of running a business.

Meanwhile, I was also managing our household (a full-time job in itself) while trying (and failing) to be a good mum to my new baby, a good wife to my husband, a good friend, sibling, daughter and person.

Life felt completely out of control and before long my mental and physical health started to deteriorate.

Extreme stress triggered anxiety. Anxiety triggered depression. Over the next 18 months I would have four miscarriages. Then, between my third and fourth miscarriage, a close friend, someone I worked alongside every day, committed suicide.

This was the last straw.

That highly reactive feeling I spoke about earlier—it became omnipresent. I was permanently on high alert waiting for the next shitty thing to happen.

There was a definite need to wrestle back some level of 'control'.

Now I think we all know life isn't perfect. And we don't expect it to be perfect. What we do expect is that whatever life decides to throw at us, we'll be able to cope with it. In other words, we expect a certain level of resilience from ourselves.

> *When we go looking for that feeling of being 'in charge' or 'in control' of our lives, what we're really after is the feeling of resilience—the ability to roll with life's ebbs and flows.*

And after a long, hard slog, I was able to get that feeling back in my life. One of the reasons it took a while was because I have a personality that can't help but self-sabotage and revert to type. I tend to move two steps forward and one step back, even when determined to effect real change in my life.

Every so often though, I managed to move three or four steps forward. And each time that happened it was because I approached things from a slightly different angle.

I found it fascinating how some of the subtlest shifts in my thinking would have the biggest effect on how I approached (and coped with) life.

Hence this book.

It's my opportunity to share those subtle shifts in thinking with you; shifts that will work for anyone.

They'll work for people who feel they're not in control of their own destiny right now. And they will work for those whose life is great, but are looking to ensure they continue to thrive.

HOW TO READ THIS BOOK

You know how a lot of people say at the start of their books "this book is designed for you to dip in and out as and when you need to?"

Well this book is designed to be read from start to finish (the first time anyway). I know! Crazy!

If you're the person this book was written for, I know you don't have a lot of time. That's why I've kept it very short—around 10,000 words. It takes most people around an hour to read so grab a cuppa ... and enjoy!

And then please feel free to dip in and out after that! Many people have told me they've read it multiple times and each time a different bit resonated.

Regardless of whether this is your first time through or your fifth, however, my hope is the same: that by the time you turn the last page you'll feel energised and ready to start putting the things that resonated most with you to good use straight away.

HERE'S WHAT ELSE I HOPE

It took me more than a year to feel I'd regained control of the direction my life was heading. More than a year to feel I was doing more than simply coping with whatever life threw at me. To feel like I was thriving.

I want it to happen a lot quicker for you.

I want your best year ever to start now, whether you're reading this in January or July. And I want each subsequent year from this point on to be your best too.

So, are you ready?

Let's do this!

CHAPTER ONE

A different way of looking at yourself

1

A significant turning point in my life came when my brother pointed out I had a superiority complex.

At first I was (naturally) indignant. How dare he? He was accusing me of thinking I was better than someone else (him specifically), and I was *not* the kind of person who thought that way.

About anyone.

But once I got past my righteous indignation, I had to admit he was right. I *did* think I was better than him.

The same way I thought I was better than people who:

- didn't share my socially-conscious, left-leaning views;
- didn't eat well or exercise;
- didn't have the same drive and determination to succeed that I did.

I clearly had a superiority complex about pretty much anything I felt smug about.

And if I look back to my high school years, I can see it there too.

When all the 'popular' people were drinking alcohol and taking drugs at parties, I wasn't. I hated to be seen as following the crowd, and felt in going left when everyone else was going right that I was better than all of them.

This carried through into adult life too. I remember first stumbling across the community of Australian bloggers on Twitter.

At the time it seemed there were four or five popular bloggers at the 'top of the tree', and everyone else was clamouring for their attention.

"Ugh," I thought. "Just like high school."

So I again decided I would *not* follow the crowd. I flat out refused to read the 'cool' bloggers' blogs or try to connect with them. Instead I found my own newbie friends and read their blogs instead. I felt it made me better than the people who seemed so desperate to get the 'popular crowd's' attention.

But of course, it didn't!

I eventually did start following those uber-popular bloggers and what did I find out? That they were popular for a good reason: they were some of the nicest, kindest, most encouraging people you'll ever meet.

I felt like such a jerk.

While school has its good points, one of its downfalls is how quickly (and early) it teaches us about life's pecking order. At the top of the tree are the people we deem 'cool'–and everyone wants to be part of the 'cool' crowd right?

Once you leave school it's pretty hard to drop that line of thinking because if we're honest with ourselves, those situations where *we* feel cool, we also tend to feel superior.

And this cancels out the times we feel inferior and *uncool*.

(How do you know if you feel inferior to someone and have decided they're 'better' than you? Well, imagine them coming up to you right now and starting a conversation with you. You'd probably spend the entire time obsessing about not saying the wrong thing because you so desperately want them to like you.

Now picture chatting with someone you feel superior to. Would you have the same problem? Probably not.)

TIME TO SHIFT YOUR THINKING

Tell yourself this: *I am no better than anyone else.*

Here's what I had to tell myself:

- My socially-conscious, left-leaning views *do not* make me any better than 'right-wing rednecks'.
- The fact that I exercise and eat well *does not* make me better than people who don't.
- The fact that I'm highly driven to achieve 'success' *does not* make me better than those people who are happy to go with the flow and float through life.

The moment I truly came to believe *I was no better than the next person*, I also realised this:

No-one else is better than me.

Do you have any idea how freeing it is when you stop looking *both up at and down on* people? When you truly look at every person on earth in equal fashion?

A dear friend of mine (who no longer graces this earth) really embodied this concept. He was a lawyer: whip-smart, quick-witted, super-interesting and very popular. His best trait, however, was that he never spoke down to anyone, not even people who were deliberately goading or infuriating him. He set a remarkable example for giving people the same level of respect and the same amount of his time, no matter who they were.

Only someone highly secure in their self-worth can achieve this, but what comes first? Respect for others or respect for yourself?

Well, if in doubt, start with respect for others. Why?

Because a magical thing happens when you start treating everyone you meet with the same amount of respect.

You start to show *yourself* more respect too.

I can't even begin to tell you how important this is from a self-worth point of view. And if there is one thing that's going to help ensure every year is your best ever, it's a rock-solid sense of self-worth.

CHAPTER TWO
A different way of looking at time

2

We've all played the "If only I had more time" game, haven't we? (Oh, the things we could achieve if only we didn't have a job, kids, family commitments, etc.)

I certainly played it when I was a triathlete.

When I was at the peak of my powers I was also working full-time. This saw me continually frustrated that so many people I competed against either worked part-time or not at all. It gnawed at me that they had all day to train and recover while I was only able to train first thing in the morning and after work in the afternoons. As for recovery, what recovery? While I was throwing down a sandwich at my desk during my lunch break they were at home with their feet up or getting a massage. Gosh that irked me!

Every time one of these people beat me in a race I felt the injustice of having to compete against people who had more time to dedicate to the sport.

These days I'm playing the same game. My goals may be more writing-centred now, but lack of time is still my main frustration. I'm a wife and a mother. I run a business and a household. And I want to do them *all* as well as I possibly can.

So I grudgingly fit my writing in where and when I can—at 5am when everyone in my house is sleeping, or in snatched half-hour blocks here and there. You can see why, when Penelope Trunk (mother, writer, entrepreneur) wrote this about a peer of hers, it really touched a nerve.

> *"Ramit doesn't have kids. He jet sets between NY and San Francisco preaching to people about fear when honestly, my biggest fear is that I can't keep up with people like Ramit who have no responsibility in their life except to grow their business. What about that fear? The fear of competing with people who don't have kids."* [1]

I allowed myself a good few days of wallowing after reading that.

If someone as successful as Penelope feels the unfairness of this situation then surely I can rail against it too? I'm tired of competing with people who don't have kids. Or whose kids are older now and less dependent on them. I have a six-year-old and a two-year-old. I see some writers going off on a writing retreat for two weeks at a time. I don't ever get even a whole *day* just to write. Poor me.

Then I remembered a lesson I learned from my triathlon days.

At one point I got to take a few weeks off work. Woo hoo! Extra time to train and recover. The chance to be a full-time athlete for a month. I couldn't wait to see how much faster I could get with all the extra training I'd get done.

But I never got to find out.

During those weeks, when my alarm went off at 5am for a 5.30am swim session I'd think, "Hey, I don't *have* to get up now. I've got all day to do this session." So I'd cancel the alarm and go back to sleep. (Actually I'd just doze fitfully for the next couple of hours. When you're used to getting up at 5am, your body actually won't let you sleep 'til 7am.)

When I finally got out of bed I'd spend a lazy hour having a coffee and reading the paper. Then my mind would turn to the session I'd missed at the pool, and how I'd have to do it by myself. I had no great love of training, so perishing the thought of doing a solo session I'd decide, "You know what? I'll just skip this one and start again tomorrow".

This pattern repeated itself for the whole month. Sometimes I'd make it to my session but mostly I wouldn't. Without boundaries dictating when I *had* to train, I really struggled. I was in a constant mental battle with myself and, not surprisingly, my performance didn't improve one iota during that period. It was only when I returned to working full-time that things started to pick up again.

Why? Because I knew there was no opportunity to make up lost sessions. So I made sure I did them.

Which brings me to four ways you can shift the way your mind thinks about time.

1. THE MORE TIME WE HAVE, THE MORE TIME WE WASTE

These days I often wake up at 4.30am because I need to produce 1000 words before 6am.

When I do, I don't make coffee, check my email or 'quickly see what everyone's up to on Facebook.' I don't have time for any of that! I have to simply open my laptop and start typing.

I don't have time for writer's block either.

Some days the words flow, and sometimes they don't. But flowing or not, I get them out. I learned a long time ago that you can edit 1000 crappy words, or find the gem in 1000 crappy words that will let you produce 1000 lovely words quick smart. But you can't do anything with a blank page.

I know writers who get to spend entire days at home writing. And yet I see them procrastinating on Twitter and Facebook—because they can.

And then I see them doing their writing at night (when I'm doing my writing!) because they've squandered their entire day and have to catch up.

So just because someone has more time to write than me doesn't necessarily mean they're writing more.

2. TIME RESTRAINTS FORCE US TO PRACTISE OUR CRAFT MORE DELIBERATELY

It might surprise you to find out that when you're trying to get better at something it's *deliberate* practice that gives the best results, not the *most* practice.

Anders Ericsson studied elite violinists. He found the best violinists weren't spending more time practising their craft, but rather practising more deliberately during their sessions. [2]

Kobe Bryant is one of the world's best basketballers. When practising shooting he doesn't set out to shoot for three hours. He sets out to make 800 shots. Once he's made his 800 shots, he's done. Total time doesn't even come into it. [3]

This is fantastic news for those of us with limited time to achieve mastery of our craft. We're not disadvantaged at all as long as we're being deliberate and productive with the time we *do* have.

3. NO-ONE HAS ENOUGH TIME TO DO EVERYTHING THEY WANT TO DO

I don't know anyone who thinks they have enough time to achieve all their goals.

Highly motivated people with lots of time on their hands tend to channel their energies into every project that captures their imagination. And of course they wish they had more time to spend on all of them.

Those of us with limited time? We're forced to be selective and pursue only the things most important to us.

Is this a bad thing? Hell no.

Our less-restricted counterparts likely know their energies are being stretched too far. But unless you're forced to, it's hard to pull back.

4. THE PEOPLE WE ENVY FOR THEIR TIME, ENVY US AS WELL

My jobless triathlon competitors probably envied the fact I never had to scrape around for cash if something on my bike broke or I had to travel interstate for a race. While Penelope is coveting Ramit's ability to focus his efforts on building his business, Ramit probably envies the fact Penelope has kids, or that she doesn't have to jump on a plane every week.

So our limited time isn't the enemy we think it is. It provides structure and boundaries to our days. It forces us to prioritise and pursue only the things most important to us. It forces us to get rid of the stuff that isn't important.

It also forces us to remember that:

The people who achieve the most aren't the ones with the most time on their hands, but the ones who waste the least of the time available to them.

For those of us looking to have our best year ever, that's huge! We can stop worrying about other people now. We can stop coveting what we think they have (soooo much time).

We can focus on just one thing. Wasting less of the available hours in our own days.

CHAPTER THREE

A different way to approach decision making

3

A few years ago my husband and I put an offer on a house.

My husband had to be convinced it was the 'right' thing to do because he was looking for something perfect (and to him, this house wasn't perfect).

I figured the only way we'd find 'perfect' was if we built something ourselves. Plus, I was feeling the pressure of our second child's imminent birth and wanted the whole 'house issue' to be sorted before she arrived. As far as I was concerned, as long as the price was right, the house we'd found ticked all the right boxes for our soon-to-be family of four.

But in the end the price wasn't right, and our offer fell through.

One month later we found (and bought) the vacant block of our dreams. We're currently building our 'forever house' on it.

Now, what if we'd managed to buy that 'imperfect' house in the end? Would it have been the worst decision ever?

Would it have affected our future happiness?

(Because that's what decision making is all about—trying to predict the future happiness a decision will give you.)

What if I told you there's just about no such thing as a bad decision, and that pretty much any decision you make could bring future happiness? (Yes, there are obvious caveats to this, but stay with me.)

In his incredibly popular TED talk, *The surprising science of happiness*, Harvard psychologist Dan Gilbert talks about:

> *"A system of cognitive processes ... that help [humans] change their views of the world, so that they can feel better about the worlds in which they find themselves."* [4]

Gilbert calls this 'system of cognitive processes' a psychological immune system. In short, it's something we all have, something that enables us to be happy no matter what situation we find ourselves in.

With this in mind I have four shifts in thinking to offer when it comes to making decisions.

1. STOP TRYING TO AVOID REGRET

When we're agonising over something, trying to decide which of two directions to take, we're really trying to avoid the regret of one option presenting itself as 'better' after the fact.

We need to stop trying to avoid regret. Regret happens. Then our psychological immune system kicks in (if we let it!) and we quickly move on.

Yes, if my husband and I had bought that house and then found out about our dream block, there would have been regret.

But our 'imperfect' house, complete with pool, entertaining area and park across the road, would have quickly cancelled out that 'regret'. We would have congratulated ourselves for not taking on the stress of building a house and having to move in with my poor father-in-law for three years.

2. THE DIFFERENCE BETWEEN TWO POSSIBLE FUTURES IS USUALLY MUCH SMALLER THAN WE THINK

When a decision isn't clear-cut, when we're agonising between two options, it's often because the potential difference in future happiness between the two is tiny.

Do you see how ridiculous it is to tie yourself in knots trying to choose between two outcomes that will both result in a similar degree of happiness?

It's like tossing back and forth for hours whether to have the Maggie Beer Chocolate and Salted Caramel Ice-Cream, or the Burnt Fig, Honeycomb and Caramel Ice-Cream. Oh my god, they're both going to be awesome, so just choose one already!

3. THE BIGGER THE DECISION, THE MORE LIKELY YOU'LL BE HAPPY WITH IT

In *The surprising science of happiness* [4], Gilbert cites a study he constructed that showed the less reversible a decision is, the more likely you'll be happy with it. And few things are less reversible than big life decisions—moving to another country, buying a new house, changing careers, deciding to have children, etc.

Not surprisingly, these are the decisions we expend the most energy on, desperately weighing up the potential differences in future happiness they'll bring. So it's pretty good news to find out that, no matter which direction we go with these major life decisions, our future happiness will be essentially the same.

4. DO NOT SNEER AT SYNTHESISED HAPPINESS

You've probably picked up by now that humans can, and do, make their own happiness.

For some reason we think the happiness that 'happens' to us (when life is good) is superior to the happiness we make. We think that 'making the best of a bad situation' is somehow faking it.

In the introduction of this book I mentioned a couple of pretty ordinary years I had circa 2010-11. And it would be easy to say, "Of course they were crappy years. You had four miscarriages, suffered from depression and someone close to you committed suicide."

Now take a look at 2012-13.

Those two years featured nine months of crippling anxiety while pregnant with my second child. Early complications in the pregnancy didn't just further that anxiety, they meant I missed a long-anticipated overseas family holiday. We moved house one month after my daughter's birth (moving is acknowledged as one of life's most highly stressful events). Shortly after that I suffered post-natal depression. Then my beloved grandma died. I was also fighting so much with my husband about our business I wasn't sure our marriage would survive.

Yet I rate those two years as the best and happiest of my life, and I believe it's because my psychological immune system was in full flight. It let me regard the bad stuff in an almost detached fashion, like it was happening to someone else. Meanwhile, all the good stuff that was happening stayed at the top of my consciousness.

So you can stop agonising over whether the decision you're currently trying to make is going to result in future happiness. With few exceptions, the decision you make now *will* make you happy; your brain is hard-wired to ensure this is so.

CHAPTER FOUR

A different way to approach bad habits

4

The ten years I spent training and competing in triathlon gave me fairly terrible habits with regard to food, the main one being I could eat whatever I wanted, whenever I wanted.

So I did, at least eight times a day: breakfast #1, breakfast #2, morning tea, lunch, afternoon tea, pre-training snack, post-training snack and dinner. Thank goodness I went to bed at 8.30pm most nights or there would have been a post-dinner snack in there too.

By the time I finished triathlon, the habit of eating every one to two hours was deeply embedded in my daily routine. And I'd created a very strong connection between exercise and food: food was my reward for doing a lot of exercise.

So even though I was finished with triathlon, I continued to try and exercise for 20 hours a week. In my head this was what I needed to do to support my eating habit. Unsurprisingly this turned out to be unsustainable. (It's a bit hard to do 20 hours of exercise/training when you're not actually training for anything!)

Since 'eating whatever I wanted' was now no longer possible (because I couldn't do the exercise to keep up) it was clear I needed to do something different to 'get my eating under control'. So I started painstakingly counting calories, ensuring that whatever I was taking in was being expended by the exercise I was doing. This was terrible because it created an even stronger link between exercise and food in my mind.

So I tried a different tack.

Instead of attempting to control my eating habit I thought I could simply break the habit by ... well, by not doing it anymore.

Anyone who's an expert on the topic of habits will tell you **it's really, *really* hard to just get rid of a habit.** [5] The patterns of repetition we create around our habits are incredibly strong, and trying to break these patterns creates a sense of deprivation because we can no longer do or have something we're used to doing or having.

When I couldn't stay on the path of simply eating less because of the overwhelming sense of deprivation, I got very down on myself and did what everyone else does. I went looking for motivation to get me back on track.

I tried tough love. "You're not an athlete anymore, so stop acting like you can eat like one."

That worked for about a day.

I tried weighing myself every day.

That didn't work either.

It soon became clear I needed to shift my thinking about my eating habit and learn some important facts.

1. FORGET ABOUT FINDING THE MOTIVATION TO BREAK A BAD HABIT

You know what? If there's a bad habit you want to break, you rarely have a shortage of motivation to do it.

I really, really wanted to eat less. I was highly motivated to break the habit of eating all the time. So my problem wasn't motivation.

It was willpower—the ability to follow through.

Confronted with the feeling of deprivation from trying to eat fewer times a day, I simply didn't have the willpower I needed to push through.

2. BREAKING BAD HABITS IS HARD. IT'S MUCH EASIER TO MAKE NEW AND BETTER HABITS. [6]

When I thought about the way I was approaching food, I could see I'd created a strong reward loop between eating and exercise. In my head, I could eat as much as I wanted as long as I did heaps of exercise.

But as I mentioned earlier, I couldn't sustain the exercise needed to justify my eating habit. And every time I didn't do the amount of exercise needed to offset a day's worth of eating, I hated myself. My eating problem created a horrible cycle of self-loathing that got completely out of hand.

I finally figured out that what I needed to do was dissociate eating and exercise.

So I created a new habit where I ate the same (reasonable) amount of food (calorie wise) each day whether I exercised or not. Note that I didn't try and change my existing habit of eating a million times a day. When your stomach is programmed to say 'I'm hungry' every two hours, that's hard to change in the short-term.

3. SMALL STEPS

Like anyone else, when I want to make a change I want to make it BIG and I want to make it NOW. But I've learned the hard way this is a sure-fire way to fail at creating a new and better habit.

When I decided to eat a set number of calories per day, I had to do it in stages. Going straight from a silly amount of food per day to an appropriate amount of food per day would have created too great a sense of deprivation. Deprivation trumps willpower, and having your willpower overridden starts a shame spiral that drops you into a neat little mindset of self-loathing. Not nice.

So, over the course of several months, I lowered the sheer volume of food I was consuming, bit by bit. By the time I'd gotten things down to an appropriate level a happy by-product was that I'd also managed to eliminate the mindset of "Oh hey, I just ran for an hour. That deserves pizza."

Today I no longer exercise to eat. I exercise for my mind and my general health. I eat to provide fuel for my body rather than as a reward. It's a nice place to be.

Since breaking my horrible eating habit I've used these same mind shifts to create other new and better habits. Things like writing every morning, being more productive at work and drinking more water.

The beautiful thing about habits is once you create them, they're easy to maintain. **And when something is a habit, there's no need to go looking for motivation.**

This is a good thing because, as you now know, motivation is a myth.

Changing the way you approach your bad habits should have a huge impact on whether this next year is your best ever.

Bad habits create a lot of angst and make us hate ourselves. It's really hard to achieve any level of control over life when someone (you) is being mean to you all the time.

> **So create new and better habits,**
> **and give yourself a break.**

CHAPTER FIVE

A different way to face your fears

5

What would you do if you weren't scared?

In 2012 I wrote a few blog posts about my journey towards living A Life Less Frantic® and they really seemed to resonate with my readers. I'd been wanting to write a book for a long time, and the response to those blog posts suggested I had something I could write a book about (i.e. how being a typically Type A, serial over-achiever and dedicated people pleaser led me into a giant hole where taking my own life seemed like the only way out).

So I started to write.

Then, about 1000 words in I stopped cold, gripped with fear.

And fear found a voice.

Who do you think you are, Kelly? You realise you're writing a memoir, right? Who are you to be writing a memoir? The world doesn't need your story. This is just pure indulgence.

That fear, and its close cousin self-doubt, stopped me in my tracks for days before I realised it was completely in my power to tell them to shut the hell up.

So I did just that.

I started back writing and a few months later I finished the book.

Was it good enough to be published beyond releasing it into hands of my lovely, very invested, blog readers? No. Truth be told it *was* indulgent. And what I wrote about was very much surface stuff. Very safe. Good memoirs aren't safe.

But I now have the first draft of that book. A book I think I can eventually be proud of.

What's more, I now get to read memoirs with a completely different eye. I marvel at the detail and emotion a great memoir writer brings to their story. If I read a 'meh' memoir, I see the mistakes the writer has made, and note if I've made the same mistakes in my own first draft.

Knowledge is power, and I wouldn't know any of this if I hadn't found the courage to push through my fear and finish the book.

So what do we need to know about courage?

1. WOBBLY COURAGE IS STILL COURAGE

When we think of courage, we think of a huge and powerful emotion brave people can summon at will. With this level of courage I would have stood up to the voice of my fears, stared down my self-doubts and ninja kicked them into 2018 like Chuck Norris.

But that's not what I did.

In 2013 I attended a conference where Darren Rowse (Problogger) discussed the concept of 'wobbly courage'. And I realised that's what I used to write my book.

I was definitely no Chuck Norris.

I wobbled. Big time.

But then I pushed on.

Maybe it helped that I'd once let the voice in my head ruin things for me.

In 2002, I competed in triathlon at the Manchester Commonwealth Games for Trinidad and Tobago (the country where I was born and lived until I was nine).

Had I been living in Trinidad at the time I would have attended those Games with my head held high, proud to represent my country as their best female triathlete. But I'd lived in Australia for years, had done all my triathlon development and racing there, and I was a long way away from being *Australia's* best female triathlete.

So instead of enjoying the experience of competing at a major Games for the country of my birth, (and where a lot of my family still lives), I spent the whole time scared someone would come up to me and say, "You don't belong here. Go home."

It turned out the only person I needed to be scared of was myself. What a waste of an amazing experience.

I really wish I knew about wobbly courage back then.

2. WE NEED TO START THINKING, "WHAT'S THE BEST THAT CAN HAPPEN?"

In the keynote I mentioned previously, Darren also spoke about how we try to overcome our fears by asking ourselves, "What's the worst that could happen?" Our instinct for self-preservation is pretty strong, isn't it?

So what is the worst that could happen? Death?

Ruining our family financially? Breaking up with our partner?

I agree all these things are bad. But they rarely apply to the things we want to try. More often than not we're scared that:

- People will think we're full of ourselves.
- Our thing won't work out so well, and others will see us as a failure.
- We'll pour our heart and soul into something only to have people laugh at us.

Isn't it sad that, a lot of the time, our fears can be boiled down to what other people might think about us?

Now I'm not going to suggest you simply stop caring about what other people think about you. I realise I may as well tell you to stop breathing.

Instead, try focusing on the best that could happen if you push through your fear.

With that book I wrote, here was some of the best stuff that could happen:

> *"I sat down with a coffee to read a chapter or two of your book, and two hours later found myself still reading."*

> *"Your book really made me have a good think about the way I am living my life/the path I am on."*
>
> *"I really saw myself in your book ... and it made me stop and think."*

I didn't know I'd get emails saying those things when I was writing that book, but I won't pretend they weren't part of my 'best things that could happen' scenario. And happily, some of that scenario played out.

What if it didn't? Well sure, I would have been crushed. But I would have learned from the experience and moved on because ...

3. THERE IS NO SUCH THING AS FAILURE

We've all seen the Internet memes about 'famous failures'.

> *Kentucky Fried Chicken's* **Harland David Sanders (Colonel Sanders)** *had his 'finger licking' good chicken recipe rejected more than 1000 times before it was finally accepted by a restaurant.*

> **Thomas Edison** is famous for inventing the lightbulb. But we don't hear much about the 1000 unsuccessful prototypes he created before coming up with the design that worked.
>
> **Stephen King's** book Carrie was knocked back by publishers 30 times, and he actually threw it in the trash. Thankfully his wife got him to fish it out and re-submit it, as it has now sold millions of copies and is considered an icon.
>
> **Abraham Lincoln,** one of the greatest Presidents of the USA, was twice declared bankrupt and was defeated in 26 early campaigns for public office.

Now it's admittedly quite easy to look back on failure from the lofty heights of success. It is, however, a lot harder to deal with it when it's actually happening.

I've found the best way to deal with failure (especially when you're in the thick of it) is to pretend there's no such thing.

And really, there isn't.

I've tried lots of things in my lifetime. Some worked out, and some didn't. But instead of dwelling on the things that didn't work out, I learned from them and moved on.

If that sounds overly simplistic, well that's because it *is*. Simple, that is.

We overthink a lot of stuff in life, and the concept of failure is one of these things. We spend far too much time wishing we hadn't tried something that didn't work out instead of being happy we can cross that thing off our list.

"Tried it. Didn't work. What's next?"

I mentioned regret in an earlier chapter, and what I said there applies just as equally here.

Regret happens. Acknowledge it, then move on.

It's time to activate your wobbly courage because nothing ruins a good year more than letting fear rule your life.

CHAPTER SIX

Changing our definition of a 'connected' life

6

As an introvert at the extreme end of the spectrum, social media has had the most amazing impact on my life.

I find it mind-blowing that I can connect with like-minded people, influencers in my industry, thought leaders, potential mentors and the tribes I'm part of without even leaving home. And from an energy point of view (we introverts need lots of time alone to re-energise and recharge), I love being able to interact with someone in a meaningful way without having to talk to them one-on-one.

But a little while ago I learned that no matter how amazing social media and the online world is, nothing beats the connection you make with people when sitting face-to-face.

Energised and inspired by a conference I'd been to, I signed up to go to a networking dinner. On my own.

Something I wouldn't normally do in oh, a million years.

Not only that, the only other person coming to the dinner who I 'knew' (well, chatted to online) was hosting it. So I was pretty sure she wouldn't be there to hold my hand throughout the ordeal ... er, experience.

The day of the dinner rolled around, and in typical fashion I started making excuses as to why I shouldn't be going. I was tired. I'd had a full-on week. I should stay home and help my husband with the kids. But in the end I summoned every bit of wobbly courage in my body and made my way to the restaurant.

When I arrived I paused on the threshold, fighting the urge to turn around and head straight home. (Now might be a good time to mention that as well as being extremely introverted I'm also stupendously shy.)

But I didn't turn around. I went in to that dinner.

And the result of the night? I found myself sitting with four amazing women. One, I'd only ever spoken to via social media and the occasional email. Another was someone I sort of knew from Twitter. And I'd never even seen the other two women before, let alone met them.

But I clicked with them all instantly, and had a great night.

Here's how that one night shifted my thinking about connecting with people.

It showed me that:

Nothing—NOTHING can replace the connection you make with people when you interact one-on-one.

In the conversations I had with those four women we shared thoughts, ideas and feelings that could never be conveyed in 140 characters, a Facebook post, or even an email. We connected at a level that is only possible when you are able to see a person's eyes and observe their body language and non-verbal reactions.

And I realised that for the past few years I'd been kidding myself a bit.

I now consider a lot of people I've met through social media as friends, even though I've never met them in real life. And I love how I can be friends with them on my own terms, dipping in and out of interacting with them as and when I feel like it.

But with the benefit of retrospect, I can see I took the whole online thing way too far. It's clear I fell into the trap of using social media as a substitute for real-life interaction with everyone in my life—including my 'real life' friends.

Everyone has a lot going on, and I often catch myself thinking, "Well, if I can't catch up with my friends in real life at least Facebook lets me keep tabs on what they're up to." And sure, yes, Facebook lets you do that.

But most of my closest friends live within 10km of my house. So the fact that I'm busy/they're busy isn't really a valid reason for not catching up. The truth is, I don't make visiting them a priority.

And when we *do* catch up and have a proper conversation, it really hit home how disconnected I was, and how little I knew about what was going on in their lives.

WHY IS IT IMPORTANT TO CONNECT WITH PEOPLE IN REAL LIFE?

Because happiness studies show human beings need face-to-face contact with other human beings. [7] Even hard-core introverts like me.

Melissa Nilles sums it up pretty well in a blog post for The Bottom Line:

> *"Ten texts can't even begin to equal an hour spent chatting with a friend over lunch. And a smiley-face emoticon is cute, but it could never replace the ear-splitting grin and smiling eyes of one of your best friends. Face time is important, people. We need to see each other."* [8]

So these days, I make it more of a priority to catch up with people in real life. And if you want to make every year your best ever, it needs to be a priority for you too.

CHAPTER SEVEN
A different way to approach your life

7

What kind of person do you think you are?

- Do you think you're a bit of a screw-up?

- Do you think you're a bit too 'soft' to ever run a business successfully?

- Do you think you're 'all talk, no action'? Overly emotional? A loose cannon?

Now ask yourself: are these your words ... or the words of others?

If there's one mistake us humans make repeatedly, it's the way we allow other people to control our destinies by letting their thoughts and expectations define us.

The only problem is, it's a rare person indeed who can push back against other people's expectations. Usually they only manage it after receiving some level of permission—from a parent, mentor, partner ... anyone but themselves.

How do you overcome this? Well first you need to stop seeking permission. Then you need to remember:

The only person who should get to decide who you are is you.

How?

Here's an idea I borrowed from James Altucher (then bastardised) that works for me.

Make a list of all the words people use to describe you, and that you use to describe yourself.

Once your list is complete, **cross off** the words you don't like. The words you think either don't apply to you, or *don't* want to apply to you.

Now **add** the words/phrases you *do* want to apply to you. Words people may not use right now, but you'd like them to use.

Now go and be that person.

"Oh, Kelly. You make it sound so easy, but it's not."

Yep, I hear you. But I'll tell you right now, it *is* that easy.

It's *highly* unlikely you've written down a trait that doesn't already live somewhere inside of you. That person you've defined? That person you want to be? That's your 'best self', someone who's probably been sitting dormant for a while, dying to get out.

So it's time to let them out! How? By changing your thinking.

Let's say (for example) you really struggled in the school system. Let's say you were a person teachers said 'would never amount to anything'.

Are you going to let yourself be defined by what you did and didn't do at school? School is a long way from the real world, and that's where you're living now. Now *you* get to decide that you're:

- *smart, focused, and someone who makes things happen;* or

- *spiritual, connected, and someone who is changing the world;* or

- *talented, hard-working, and someone who will be successful at whatever they put their mind to.*

Or whoever it is you want to be.

The words you want people to use to describe you will tell you what you want to achieve. And once you know what you want to achieve, it's completely within your power to get yourself there.

I've written countless words in my lifetime. Short stories, letters to pen pals, letters to my parents when they were fighting with each other, letters to my parents when I was fighting with them, school reports, articles, blog posts, birthday cards, sales copy, website text, the list goes on. And yet, until a few years ago, I'd never called myself a writer.

At some point I'd decided that I needed to be published in a certain number of magazines, or to have released my first book, or for other people to call me a writer before I could 'legitimately' wear that title. I think I'd also decided there needed to be an official ceremony, complete with marching band and go-go girls.

Then I read Jeff Goins' book, *You Are a Writer (So Start Acting Like One)* [9], and its core message was exactly what the title promised. Ten seconds after finishing it I put 'Writer' on my business card, website and email footer. I started thinking of myself as a writer. Most importantly, I started doing something that's key to being a writer.

I started writing every day.

Here's another time I had to re-write the story I was telling myself.

In 2010 I walked away from my business and left my husband in charge. On that day the words I used to describe myself were "*completely useless businesswoman*".

This line of thinking was given strength by the fact that, once in charge, my husband (with zero graphic design experience) turned our business financials completely around. Within six months we had positive cash flow—something we'd never had before and something most small businesses only dream of. We were able to move to nicer offices and pay our staff what they were worth. The business had money in the bank for the first time. It was kind of embarrassing.

Three years later when I returned to the office, the narrative in my head was rock-solid; I was hopeless at running a business. This was problematic because that's precisely what I was supposed to be doing on my return (in partnership with my husband).

And the negative story I was telling myself manifested in all kinds of fun ways for the people around me.

I was overly defensive and combative every time someone challenged my thoughts on something. I'd express strong opinions about how certain situations were handled when I didn't have the full story. I'd constantly test my husband to see if he thought I was an asset to the business.

Before long we were fighting all the time and I decided he didn't respect me. Not as a business partner and not as a wife.

Things were obviously getting out of hand.

I had to stop looking to my husband to verify my value. **I had to believe it of myself.**

Who did I want to be? I wanted to be a successful businesswoman. I wanted to be someone who brought significant value to our business.

So I changed the story I was telling myself.

I reminded myself that I was *someone people really liked doing business with.*

That's not to say this isn't true for my husband. He's a nice person but his strengths lie in systems and processes. My strengths are with people. A successful business requires equal focus on *both* these things so it quickly became clear that I was as valuable to our business as my husband was.

Needless to say, once I changed the story in my head, things righted themselves for us, both in the office and at home.

So in the same way I asked myself the question: "Who do I WANT to be?", it's time to ask it of yourself too.

Remember, the only person who should get to write the story of your life is you. So start shaping a narrative around the person you want to be, not the person other people think you are (or the person you've been telling yourself you are).

SO WHAT NOW?

I can hear you thinking "Agh, we're done already? Where's my direction? Where do I go from here?"

So let's start with a quick recap. Here are the seven damaging thoughts I've discussed in this book that stop you from feeling like you're thriving:

1. In this world there are people who I am better than, and there are people who are better than me.

2. I don't have the time I need to achieve my goals.

3. The thought of making a bad decision paralyses me. And often results in me doing nothing.

4. I have a bad habit that makes me hate myself because I can't break it.

5. Fear of what people will think of me stops me from pursuing things I am passionate about.

6. Isn't Facebook great? It allows me to stay in touch with my friends without the need to see them in person.

7. I don't feel I have permission to be myself. I feel I'm living a life defined by the negative perception I have of myself or that others have of me.

What do these seven damaging thoughts add up to? They are things that get in the way of you being your best self. They are things that chip away at the foundation of your self-worth.

And what experience has taught me is that you will really struggle to ride out the ebbs and flows of life without a rock-solid platform of self-worth.

So how are you going to turn around your thinking about those seven things? Well you're going to realise:

1. You're no better than anyone else in this world, and no-one is better than you. People who truly understand this develop a huge respect for everyone they come across in life. And most importantly they develop a huge respect for themselves too.

2. No-one has the time they need to achieve all their goals. The people who achieve the most in life are the ones who waste the least of the time they have.

3. There is no such thing as a bad decision. Whatever you end up deciding, that's the right decision because you are hard-wired to make it so. Also, the more you're agonising between two things, the more likely either choice will bring you equal future happiness.

4. It's almost impossible to break a bad habit. This is why you need to develop new and better habits instead.

5. You don't need huge amounts of courage to surmount your fears. You need only the smallest amount of wobbly courage.

6. Humans need face-to-face contact with other humans. Online interaction simply cannot replicate the depth of understanding, meaning and connection you get from speaking with another person face-to-face.

7. You need to stop looking for permission. The only person who gets to decide who you are and what kind of person you are ... is you.

Getting your head around these little shifts in thinking will add up to something big. And that something big is self-worth.

Why is self-worth so important?

Let's be honest: in life, bad stuff happens to nice people. And there's not much we can do to control how and when that stuff happens. What we *can* control, however, is how we react to life's challenges.

That's where self-worth comes into the picture.

Self-worth is a shield that activates when 'stuff' - big or small - threatens to rock your world.

When that shield is at full power *you too* are at full power.

And it's that power that's going to help make every year from here on your best ever.

THE END

REFERENCES AND CREDITS

1. ***Five steps to make a breakdown just a little breakdown***, Penelope Trunk, blog.penelopetrunk.com/2013/12/09/five-steps-to-make-a-breakdown-just-a-little-breakdown/

2. **The Role of Deliberate Practice in the Acquisition of Expert Performance**, K. Anders Ericsson, Ralf Th. Krampe, and Clemens Tesch-Romer, Psychological Review 1993, Vol. 100. No. 3, 363-406

3. **What Mozart and Kobe Bryant Can Teach Us About Deliberate Practice,** James Clear, lifehacker.com/what-mozart-and-kobe-bryant-can-teach-us-about-delibera-1442488267

4. **The surprising science of happiness,** Dan Gilbert, www.ted.com/talks/dan_gilbert_asks_why_are_we_happy

5. **Breaking Bad Habits: Why It's So Hard to Change,** Vicki Contie, www.nlm.nih.gov/medlineplus/magazine/issues/spring12/articles/spring12pg18-19.html

6. ***How to Break a Bad Habit (and Replace It With a Good One),*** James Clear, *jamesclear.com/how-to-break-a-bad-habit*

7. **Face-to-face contact with close happy family and friends is good for boosting happiness**, Nyomi Graef, *extrahappiness.com/happiness/?p=2232*

8. **Technology is Destroying the Quality of Human Interaction,** Melissa Nilles, *thebottomline.as.ucsb.edu/2012/01/technology-is-destroying-the-quality-of-human-interaction*

9. **You Are a Writer (So Start Acting Like One),** Jeff Goins, *www.youareawriter.com*

ACKNOWLEDGEMENTS

To Bernadette Jiwa and Alexx Stuart – the impetus to get off my butt and write this book started with you. Thank you for the inspiration, advice and cheerleading.

To Bill Harper, my sharp-eyed editor – you take my convoluted sentences and make them trim and sparkly. Such a gift.

To Kym Campradt, my eagle-eyed proof-reader, for picking up all the dodgy stuff I did to Bill's lovely editing!

To my wonderful beta readers/guinea pigs: Jan Exeter, Robyn Petta, Rory Mouttet, Holly Kent, Anna Hill, Sarah Pietrzak and Anna Spargo-Ryan – your feedback was invaluable and has made this book 100% better than the first version you saw.

To Karen Taylor – all I can say is thank goodness for you! You helped shape the most important part of this book and everyone who reads it owes you one.

And finally, to Anthony Exeter who makes me a better person every single day. And to Jaden and Mia, because everything I do, I do for you.

THANK YOU

As a fellow reader with limited time on my hands, I know what it's like to commit to a book, long or short. If you've got this far, I'm honoured and appreciative that you've gifted your time to me. I hope you enjoyed *Your Best Year Ever.*

If you did, please drop me an email at kelly@kellyexeter.com.au; I find it so interesting to hear which bits particularly resonated as it seems to be different for everyone.

And if you'd like to stay in touch, I'd love that too! You can:

Get weekly tips for living A Life Less Frantic® at kellyexeter.com.au

Say hi on Facebook (facebook.com/kellyexeter) or Twitter (@kellyexeter)

Thank you again!

Kelly x

www.ingramcontent.com/pod-product-compliance
Lightning Source LLC
Chambersburg PA
CBHW051956290426
44110CB00015B/2262